LEADERSHIP

IS

HUMAN

The EQ Superpower—How
Emotionally Intelligent Leaders
Elevate Performance, People and
Impact in the Age of AI

TENA H. SLOAN

Human Potential Partners

Published by Human Potential Partners, LLC
San Jose, CA, USA

ISBN-13: 979-8-9928164-0-2

Printed in the United States of America
First Edition

For more information, visit:
www.leadershipishumanbook.com

DEDICATION

To my daughter, Avery—your creativity, curiosity, and boundless spirit inspire me to push beyond my limits, embrace possibility, and remain grounded in gratitude. You are my greatest teacher.

To my teachers, mentors, colleagues, past managers, and those I have had the privilege to lead —this book is also for you. The lessons, insights, and wisdom shared within were shaped by both our triumphs and our challenges. Every success, every setback, and every moment of growth has been a part of this journey.

Thank you for the experiences that have made this work possible.

Table of Contents

Introduction:
Leadership is Human – The EQ Superpower That Transforms Leadership in the Age of AI

The landscape of leadership is undergoing a seismic shift. In an era defined by artificial intelligence, rapid automation, and unprecedented workplace disruption, traditional leadership models are no longer enough. The leaders who will thrive in the modern age are not those who simply manage tasks or enforce authority— they are the ones who inspire, connect, and lead with emotional intelligence (EQ).

For decades, leadership has been associated with strategic thinking, decision-making, and operational execution. While these skills remain essential, they are no longer the sole drivers of success. The real differentiator in leadership today, and in the future, is emotional intelligence.

Why? Because people drive organizations forward, and in a world where technology is accelerating change, human connection, trust, and influence are more critical than ever. The leaders who understand and leverage this EQ superpower will outperform, inspire, and thrive, while those who ignore it will struggle to keep up.

This book is about why and how emotional intelligence transforms leadership, not as a nice-to-have soft skill, but as the defining superpower of modern leaders who seek to create impact, lead resilient teams, and drive meaningful change in the age of AI.

The Leadership Shift: Why Emotional Intelligence Matters More Than Ever

Leadership is at a crossroads. Workplaces are experiencing:

• **A Mental Health Crisis:** Burnout, stress, and disengagement are at all-time highs. Leaders who fail to prioritize mental well-being will see their teams struggle to perform and innovate.

• **The Rise of AI and Automation:** While artificial intelligence is revolutionizing industries, it cannot replace human connection, emotional intelligence, and the ability to inspire people.

• **A Demand for Human-Centered Leadership:** Employees and organizations are rejecting outdated leadership models in favor of leaders who prioritize people, purpose, and impact over rigid systems and short-term gains.

• **The Unpredictability of Change:** Crisis, market disruptions, and uncertainty require leaders who can adapt, communicate with emotional intelligence, and foster resilience in themselves and their teams.

The old command-and-control leadership playbook has expired. The leaders who succeed today are those who know how to cultivate trust, create psychologically safe workplaces, and elevate the potential of their people.

The future of leadership is human-centered. It is about leading with awareness, empathy, and adaptability, the key ingredients of emotional intelligence.

The EQ Superpower: Your Competitive Advantage in Leadership

Great leadership is not just about what you do, it is about how you make people feel and how you show up in the moments that matter. Research consistently shows that leaders with high EQ:

• Outperform their counterparts in leadership effectiveness and business impact.

• Build stronger, more engaged teams that trust, collaborate, and innovate together.

• Foster psychological safety, creating environments where people feel safe to contribute and take risks.

• Navigate conflict, difficult conversations, and workplace challenges with empathy and influence.

• Lead with clarity, confidence, and composure in high-pressure situations.

• Drive organizational success by aligning human

potential with business strategy.

This book will show you how to develop, refine, and leverage your EQ superpower to become the kind of leader who does not just manage tasks, but transforms teams, organizations, and industries.

Why This Book? Why Now?

This book is your practical road map to mastering emotionally intelligent leadership. It is actionable, strategic, and designed for real-world impact. This book will equip you with:

• The five core components of emotional intelligence and how they directly impact leadership effectiveness.

• The connection between mental health, psychological safety, and trust, the building blocks of high-performing teams.

• Influence and communication strategies that inspire action, collaboration, and commitment.

• Practical tools for resolving conflicts, leading through change, and fostering resilience.

• Self-reflection exercises, leadership challenges, and real-world case studies to turn insight into action.

This is not a book filled with abstract theories. It is a guide to becoming the kind of leader who thrives in complexity, connects with people on a deeper level, and leads with intelligence, empathy, and impact.

Who This Book is For

Leadership is Human is written for:

• **Leaders at all levels:** CEOs, managers, team leaders, and aspiring leaders who want to harness emotional intelligence to elevate their leadership.

• **Entrepreneurs and business owners:** Leaders who want to build people-first cultures that drive long-term success.

• **HR and people-focused professionals:** Individuals responsible for shaping organizational culture, employee engagement, and leadership development.

• **Anyone committed to personal and professional growth:** Leadership is not about titles; it is about influence, impact, and the ability to create positive change.

If you are committed to leading with greater emotional intelligence, navigating challenges with confidence, and building a career or business rooted in human-centered leadership, this book is for you.

The Transformation Journey Ahead

This book is more than a guide. It is a transformational journey to mastering emotional intelligence (EQ) and integrating it into your leadership approach. In an era of rapid change and AI-driven disruption, leaders who cultivate EQ will not only navigate uncertainty but also create lasting impact.

Each chapter builds on the last, offering a progressive, practical framework for developing self-awareness, fostering meaningful connections, and leading with confidence and adaptability. Through real-world strategies, case studies, and actionable exercises, you will gain the tools to apply what you learn in real time.

Part 1: Mastering Emotional Intelligence and Self Leadership
Before leading others effectively, leaders must first lead themselves. This section explores self-awareness, self-regulation, and emotional resilience in high-pressure environments.

• Chapter 1: The Human Side of Leadership—Why Emotional Intelligence Matters More Than Ever

• Chapter 2: The Five Superpowers of Emotional Intelligence in Leadership

• Chapter 3: Psychological Safety and Trust—The Bedrock of High-Performing Teams

Part 2: The Building Blocks of Human-Centered Leadership
Emotionally intelligent leadership extends beyond personal mastery, it requires creating an environment where people can thrive.

• Chapter 4: Leading Through Change and Uncertainty with Emotional Intelligence

• Chapter 5: Conflict Resolution and Effective Communication

Part 3: The Power of Influence, Communication, and Leadership Presence
Leaders who inspire action and drive meaningful change master influence and presence.

• Chapter 6: Building a Human-Centered Leadership Culture

• Chapter 7: Leading with Authenticity and Ethical Leadership

• Chapter 8: The Path to Emotionally Intelligent Leadership

Part 4: Leading Through Change, Crisis, and Uncertainty
In today's world, leaders must be adaptive, resilient, and able to inspire confidence during times of crisis.

• Chapter 9: The Future of Human-Centered Leadership

• Chapter 10: Bringing It All Together – Your Human-Centered Leadership Road Map

Part 5: The Long-Term EQ Leadership Strategy
Leadership is not about a single moment. It is about continuous growth and leaving a lasting impact.

Conclusion: The Future of Human-Centered Leadership

Your Leadership Evolution Starts Now

Leadership is not about managing processes, it's about elevating people. If you are ready to build high-trust teams, navigate complexity with confidence, and lead with intelligence, empathy, and vision, this journey starts now.

Let's begin.

Chapter 1:

The Human Side of Leadership—Why Emotional Intelligence Matters More Than Ever

This chapter explores:

• What Emotional intelligence (EQ) is and why it is a game-changer in leadership.

• The five core components of EQ and how they impact leadership effectiveness.

• The science behind EQ and its direct connection to leadership performance.

• The difference between high-EQ leaders and low-EQ leaders.

• How mastering EQ provides a competitive advantage in leadership.

• Self-reflection exercises to assess your current EQ strengths and areas for growth.

The Evolution of Leadership: Why EQ is the Game-Changer

"Before you are a leader, success is all about growing yourself. When you become a leader, success is all about growing others." – Jack Welch

Leadership is evolving.

For decades, leadership was defined by power, expertise, and authority. The best leaders were those who made the biggest decisions, commanded respect, and controlled outcomes. But in today's complex, fast-changing world, these qualities are no longer enough.

The command-and-control leadership model is breaking down. Employees are demanding more than just direction, they want trust, psychological safety, and meaningful engagement. Teams no longer follow leaders simply because of title or rank; they follow those who demonstrate empathy, authenticity, and emotional intelligence.

Research consistently shows that leaders with high emotional intelligence (EQ) outperform those who rely solely on intellect or technical skills. Why? Because leadership is not just about what you know; it is about how you connect, inspire, and empower others.

The Bottom Line: The best leaders do not just manage

people, but they build relationships, cultivate trust, and create environments where people feel seen, valued, and motivated to contribute their best work.

The Science of Emotional Intelligence in Leadership

Emotional intelligence is the ability to recognize, understand, and manage your own emotions while also being able to perceive, influence, and respond to the emotions of others.

Daniel Goleman, who pioneered the study of emotional intelligence in leadership, identified five core components of EQ that define effective leadership:

1. Self-Awareness: Understanding Your Emotions and Triggers

• The ability to recognize and understand your emotions and their impact on your thoughts, behaviors, and decisions.
• Leaders with self-awareness are reflective, open to feedback, and continuously seek personal growth.

Example: A self-aware leader notices when they are feeling frustrated before a meeting and takes steps to regulate their response instead of reacting impulsively.

2. Self-Regulation: Managing Emotions and Reactions

• The ability to control impulsive behaviors, stay

composed under pressure, and adapt to change.

• Leaders with strong self-regulation do not let negative emotions dictate their decisions or interactions.

Example: A leader facing a difficult conversation remains calm, composed, and solution-oriented rather than becoming defensive or reactive.

3. Motivation: Leading with Purpose and Resilience

• Emotionally intelligent leaders are intrinsically motivated by a greater purpose, rather than external rewards.

• They remain optimistic, resilient, and focused on long-term success even in the face of challenges.

Example: A leader facing a setback in business maintains a growth mindset and keeps their team inspired rather than dwelling on the problem.

4. Empathy: Understanding and Connecting with Others

• The ability to recognize and understand the emotions of others and respond with care and sensitivity.

• Leaders with high empathy build strong relationships, foster trust, and create psychologically safe workplaces.

Example: An empathetic leader notices when an employee is disengaged, checks in with them, and offers support rather than automatically assuming they are unmotivated, uncaring or incompetent.

5. Social Skills: Building Influence and Strong Relationships
• Emotionally intelligent leaders communicate effectively, resolve conflicts, and inspire collaboration.
• They create an inclusive, high-trust culture where people feel valued and heard.

Example: A leader skilled in social intelligence uses active listening and clear communication to navigate conflicts and drive positive outcomes.

Leaders with high emotional intelligence:
• **Foster trust and engagement** within their teams.

• **Navigate change and uncertainty** with composure.

• **Handle conflict constructively**, rather than avoiding or escalating it.

• **Inspire action and commitment**, rather than forcing compliance.

• **Make better decisions** by balancing logic with emotional insight.

Key Insight: Research shows that EQ is a stronger predictor of leadership success than IQ or technical expertise. Harvard Business Review found that 90% of high-performing leaders have strong emotional intelligence, confirming that leadership is more about human connection than raw intelligence alone.

The Science of EQ and Leadership Performance

Neuroscience shows that emotions drive decision-making, relationships, and leadership effectiveness.

• **The Brain's Emotional Center:** The limbic system governs emotions, while the prefrontal cortex regulates rational thought and decision-making. Emotionally intelligent leaders strengthen their ability to balance these two systems, ensuring they respond thoughtfully rather than react impulsively.

• **The Amygdala Hijack:** When leaders do not regulate emotions, they experience an amygdala hijack—where stress or conflict triggers an emotional overreaction, leading to poor decisions. EQ enables leaders to recognize this response and pause before reacting.

• **The Mirror Neuron Effect:** Leaders set the emotional tone for their teams. When a leader remains composed and optimistic, it directly influences the emotions and behaviors of those they lead.

Research from Harvard, Yale, and the Center for Creative Leadership shows that 90% of top-performing leaders have high emotional intelligence.

Mental Health and Leadership: The Overlooked Connection

One of the most underrated leadership skills is the ability to *recognize and manage mental and emotional well-being*—both in yourself and in your team.

Yet, many leaders ignore their own burnout, stress, and emotional exhaustion, believing that resilience means pushing through no matter what. The truth? You cannot lead others effectively if you are mentally drained, emotionally depleted, or disconnected from your own well-being.

Leaders who prioritize self-awareness, stress management, and emotional regulation create healthier, more engaged workplaces. When leaders neglect their mental health, their teams suffer—leading to increased turnover, disengagement, and toxic workplace cultures.

Practical Leadership Insight

• **Leaders set the tone:** If you neglect mental health, your team will too.

• **Workplace well-being is a leadership responsibility**, not just an HR function.

• **Burnout is contagious:** If you are constantly stressed, it will spread to your team.

Practical Application: Your First Steps Toward EQ Mastery

To begin strengthening your *emotional intelligence as a leader*, start with these foundational practices:

1. Daily Self-Awareness Check-In

Each day, take five minutes to ask yourself:

- How am I feeling right now?
- What emotions are driving my decisions today?
- How might my emotions be impacting my leadership?

The first step in emotional intelligence is *recognizing your own emotional patterns and triggers.*

2. Name and Regulate Your Emotions in Real-Time

Before reacting emotionally in a high-pressure moment:

- Pause. Name your emotion. ("I'm feeling frustrated because…").
- Breathe. Take three deep breaths to regain composure.
- *Choose* a response instead of reacting impulsively.

3. Seek Feedback on Your Emotional Impact

Ask a trusted colleague or team member:

- "How do my emotions affect the team?"
- "What is one thing I could do to improve my emotional intelligence as a leader?"

Self-awareness is powerful, but the best leaders also seek *outside perspectives* to grow.

**** High-EQ vs. Low-EQ Leaders: ****
The Clear Contrast

High-EQ Leaders

▶ Lead with self-awareness and reflection

▶ Stay calm and composed under pressure

▶ Inspire trust and psychological safety

▶ Communicate clearly and listen actively

▶ Build strong relationships and motivate teams

▶ Adapt easily to change and uncertainty

Low-EQ Leaders

▶ Lack awareness of how their emotions impact others

▶ React impulsively and let emotions dictate behavior

▶ Create a fear-based or high-stress environment

▶ Struggle to articulate thoughts and *dismiss* others' perspectives

▶ Struggle with interpersonal conflicts and low team morale

▶ Resist change and struggle with flexibility

The best leaders in today's world are not those who dominate—they are those who connect, inspire, and lead with emotional intelligence.

How EQ Creates a Competitive Advantage in Leadership

Mastering emotional intelligence gives leaders a

sustainable edge in leadership effectiveness, performance, and impact.

• Leaders with high EQ build stronger, more engaged teams. Studies show that employees are 400% less likely to leave an organization when they feel emotionally connected to leadership.

• Emotionally intelligent leaders make better decisions. They consider long-term consequences, manage stress effectively, and make sound, ethical choices.

• High-EQ leaders drive innovation. Teams perform better when psychological safety allows for creative risk-taking, problem-solving, and collaboration.

• EQ enhances influence and executive presence. Leaders who communicate with clarity, confidence, and emotional intelligence earn greater respect and trust.

Simply put, leaders who master EQ do not just survive in leadership—they thrive.

Self-Reflection: Assessing Your Emotional Intelligence

Before moving forward, take a moment to reflect on your own EQ strengths and areas for growth.

Leadership Self-Assessment: Where Do You Stand?

Rate yourself on a scale of 1 (low) to 5 (high) in the following areas:

• I am aware of my emotions and how they impact my

leadership.
- I regulate my emotions well and do not let stress dictate my decisions.
- I am intrinsically motivated and stay resilient in challenges.
- I understand and empathize with the emotions of those I lead.
- I communicate clearly, listen actively, and inspire trust.

Where did you rate yourself highest? Where did you score lower? Identifying your strengths and weaknesses is the first step toward growth.

Key Takeaways

- Emotional intelligence (EQ) is the defining superpower of modern leadership.

- The five components of EQ—self-awareness, self-regulation, motivation, empathy, and social skills—are the foundation of leadership effectiveness.

- High-EQ leaders create trust, psychological safety, and stronger teams.

- Low-EQ leaders struggle with communication, decision-making, and engagement.

- EQ is a competitive advantage that drives performance, innovation, and influence.

What's Next?

Now that we understand why EQ is the foundation of leadership, it is time to break it down further.

In the next chapter, we will explore how to develop and apply the five core components of emotional intelligence in real-world leadership situations.

Let's dive deeper into **how you can build your leadership edge through EQ.**

Chapter 2:

The Five Superpowers of Emotional Intelligence in Leadership

This chapter explores:

• A deep dive into the five core components of EQ and how they shape leadership effectiveness.

• How self-awareness and self-regulation impact decision-making and leadership presence.

• Why empathy and social intelligence are the key to building trust and influence.

• Practical strategies and exercises to strengthen emotional intelligence in leadership.

Emotional Intelligence as a Leadership Superpower

"The most effective leaders are all alike in one crucial way: They all have a high degree of emotional intelligence. It's not that IQ and technical skills are irrelevant. They do matter, but...they are the entry-level requirements for executive positions." – Daniel Goleman

Leadership is more than just making strategic decisions and driving results. It is about understanding people—yourself and those you lead.

The best leaders have mastered a *set of emotional intelligence superpowers* that allow them to navigate conflict, inspire engagement, and drive long-term success. These *five superpowers*—rooted in Daniel Goleman's research—are the foundation of emotionally intelligent leadership.

The Five Superpowers of Emotional Intelligence

Superpower 1 - Self-Awareness: The Foundation of Emotional Intelligence
The first and most critical superpower is self-awareness—the ability to recognize and understand your own emotions, triggers, and their impact on others.

Why It Matters in Leadership

• Leaders with high self-awareness make better decisions because they understand how their emotions influence judgment.

• They navigate stress more effectively because they can identify when they are emotionally overwhelmed.

• They cultivate trust by being transparent about their strengths, weaknesses, and emotions.

Practical Strategies to Build Self-Awareness

▶ **Daily Reflection:** Spend five minutes each morning or evening identifying your emotions and their root causes. Ask yourself, "What emotions did I feel today? How did they impact my leadership?"

▶ **Feedback Audit:** Ask trusted colleagues, What is one way my emotional responses affect the team?"

▶ **Emotional Labeling:** When experiencing strong emotions, pause and name them. Instead of saying "I'm frustrated," specify "I feel frustrated because my expectations were not met." This clarity enhances emotional control.

Superpower 2 - Self-Regulation: The Power of Emotional Mastery

Self-regulation is the ability to manage emotions and reactions in a way that aligns with your leadership values and goals.

Why It Matters in Leadership

• Emotionally regulated leaders stay calm under pressure and respond thoughtfully instead of reacting impulsively.

• They create a culture of stability and trust—when leaders control their emotions, their teams feel more secure.

• Leaders who regulate emotions make sound decisions because they do not let temporary frustration cloud their judgment.

Practical Strategies to Strengthen Self-Regulation

▶ **The Three-Breath Rule:** When faced with an emotionally charged situation, take three deep breaths before responding. This interrupts impulsive reactions.

▶ **Pause Before Replying:** If an email or conversation triggers frustration, step away for five minutes before responding.

▶ **Reframe Negative Thoughts:** Instead of thinking "This setback is terrible," shift to "What can I learn from this?"

Superpower 3 -. Motivation: The Driving Force of Leadership Success

Motivation is the internal drive to lead with purpose, resilience, and long-term vision—even when challenges arise.

Why It Matters in Leadership

• Highly motivated leaders inspire teams to push beyond obstacles and stay engaged in their work.

• They maintain a growth mindset, seeing failures as opportunities for learning.

• Leaders with strong motivation model resilience, creating a culture of perseverance.

Practical Strategies to Strengthen Motivation

▶ **Reconnect with Your Leadership Why:** Write down why you lead. Revisit this statement during challenging times.

▶ **Adopt a Growth Mindset:** Instead of "I failed," think "I learned something valuable for next time."

▶ **Surround Yourself with Purpose-Driven People:** Engage with leaders who inspire and challenge you.

Superpower 4 - Empathy: The Key to Connection and Influence
Empathy is the ability to understand, relate to, and respond to the emotions of others—and it is one of the most powerful leadership skills.

Why It Matters in Leadership

• Empathetic leaders build trust and loyalty because their teams feel understood and valued.

• They anticipate team needs, leading to higher engagement and retention.

• Empathy allows leaders to navigate difficult conversations with care and effectiveness.

Practical Strategies to Develop Empathy

▶ **Listen Without Interrupting:** In your next one-on-one meeting, practice listening fully before responding.

▶ **Ask Open-Ended Questions:** Instead of "D you finish

the project?" try "What challenges did you face while working on the project?"

▶ **Walk in Their Shoes:** When an employee struggles, pause and ask, "How would I feel in their position?"

Superpower 5 - Social Skills: The Art of Leadership Communication
Social skills encompass relationship-building, influence, and communication—all of which drive leadership success.

Why It Matters in Leadership
• Leaders with strong social skills navigate conflict effectively without damaging relationships.

• They motivate and inspire teams through clear and engaging communication.

• They create inclusive, high-trust cultures where collaboration thrives.

Practical Strategies to Strengthen Social Skills
▶ **Master Active Listening:** In your next conversation, focus entirely on the speaker—no distractions. Summarize what they said before responding.

▶ **Lead with Questions:** Instead of directing every discussion, ask, "What are your thoughts on this?"

▶ **Improve Nonverbal Communication:** Maintain eye contact, use open body language, and mirror the tone of your audience to build connection.

How the Five Superpowers Work Together

These five emotional intelligence superpowers are not isolated skills, they fuel and reinforce each other:

• **Self-awareness** enhances **self-regulation**. You can not manage emotions you do not recognize.

• **Motivation** keeps leaders focused on growth, ensuring they apply **self-regulation and empathy**.

• **Empathy and social skills** build strong relationships, making it easier to **lead with influence** rather than authority.

Together, these five superpowers form the foundation of human-centered leadership, allowing leaders to create **psychologically safe, engaged, and high-performing teams**.

Practical Application: Strengthen Your EQ in 30 Days

For the next 30 days, commit to practicing one of these EQ-building strategies daily:

Week 1: Build Self-Awareness - Keep a journal of daily emotions and triggers.

Week 2: Strengthen Self-Regulation - Practice the Three-Breath Rule before responding in stressful moments.

Week 3: Cultivate Empathy - Ask one open-ended question per day to deepen understanding in conversations.

Week 4: Improve Social Skills - Lead one conversation per day with active listening and engagement.

Small, consistent actions lead to massive leadership transformation.

Key Takeaways

• Self-awareness, self-regulation, motivation, empathy, and social skills are the five superpowers of emotional intelligence in leadership.

• EQ allows leaders to navigate challenges, build trust, and inspire action.

• Each of these five components is trainable and can be strengthened over time.

• Practical exercises like emotional journaling, deep listening, and reframing negative thoughts accelerate EQ growth.

What's Next?

Now that we have explored the five superpowers of emotional intelligence, the next step is applying EQ to real-world leadership challenges.

In the next chapter, we will dive into psychological safety and trust—two critical elements that determine whether teams thrive or struggle.

Are you ready to build a **high-trust, high-performance leadership culture?**

Let's continue the journey.

Chapter 3:

Psychological Safety and Trust—The Bedrock of High-Performing Teams

This chapter explores:

• Why psychological safety and trust are essential for leadership effectiveness.

• The difference between high-trust and low-trust workplace cultures.

• How leaders unintentionally erode trust and how to rebuild it.Practical strategies to create a psychologically safe environment where teams thrive.

The Leadership Currency: Psychological Safety and Trust

"A culture of trust gives people the confidence to take risks, speak up, and share ideas—this is where innovation thrives." — Satya Nadella

Leadership is not about title or position—it's about the environment you create. Employees do not give their best to leaders they do not trust. They give the bare minimum.

When people do not feel safe to share ideas, admit mistakes, or take risks, organizations stagnate. Psychological safety and trust unlock innovation, engagement, and high performance—but they don't happen by accident.

As a leader, **your actions set the tone**. The question is: *Are you building a culture of safety and trust, or unknowingly eroding it?*

The Difference Between High-Trust and Low-Trust Cultures

High-trust environments drive engagement, creativity, and collaboration, while low-trust cultures breed fear, disengagement, and inefficiency.

* * * High-Trust vs. Low-Trust Cultures: * * *
The Clear Contrast

Low-Trust Culture

▶ Employees hesitate to speak up

▶ Fear of making mistakes

▶ Limited innovation & risk-taking

▶ Toxicity, gossip, and blame

▶ High turnover & disengagement

High-Trust Culture

▶ Employees feel safe sharing ideas & concerns

▶ Mistakes are seen as learning opportunities

▶ High creativity & problem-solving

▶ Open, respectful communication

▶ Strong retention & engagement

Trust is a competitive advantage—organizations that cultivate it outperform those that do not.

What Erodes Psychological Safety? (And How Leaders Fix It)

Even well-intentioned leaders unknowingly destroy trust in subtle ways. Recognizing these behaviors is the first step to creating a safer, stronger team environment.

1. Unclear Expectations Create Anxiety

- **What Erodes Trust:** Employees feel uncertain about what is expected of them.
- **How to Fix It:** Be clear on goals, feedback, and accountability. Say, *"Here is what success looks like for this project."*

2. Micromanagement Kills Confidence
- **What Erodes Trust:** Over-controlling leaders signal, *"I do not trust you to handle this."*
- **How to Fix It:** Give autonomy. Instead of **telling** employees what to do, ask, *"What is your plan for this?"*

3. Punishing Mistakes Stifles Learning
- **What Erodes Trust:** Employees fear speaking up because failure leads to blame.
- **How to Fix It:** Shift from punishment to growth mindset. Say, *"What did we learn from this?"*

4. Withholding Feedback Creates Uncertainty
- **What Erodes Trust:** Leaders avoid tough conversations, leaving employees guessing.
- **How to Fix It:** Give clear, honest feedback regularly. Constructive criticism builds trust when delivered with respect.

5. Inconsistency Breeds Distrust
- **What Erodes Trust:** Saying one thing but doing another confuses employees.
- **How to Fix It:** Align words with actions. If you value

work-life balance, do not email employees at midnight.

The 4 Pillars of Psychological Safety

To build a culture of safety and trust, leaders must focus on *four key pillars.*

Pillar 1: Inclusion Safety (*"I Belong Here."*)

Employees feel respected, valued, and accepted for who they are.

- **Action Step:** Encourage diverse perspectives. Say, *"I'd love to hear your take on this."*

Pillar 2: Learner Safety (*"It is Safe to Grow Here."*)

Employees feel **comfortable asking questions and making mistakes** without fear.

- **Action Step:** Model learning. Say, *"I do not have all the answers—let's figure it out together."*

Pillar 3: Contributor Safety (*"My Work Matters Here."*)

Employees feel empowered to take initiative and contribute ideas.

- **Action Step:** Give meaningful ownership. Say, *"I trust your judgment on this decision."*

Pillar 4: Challenger Safety (*"I Can Speak Up Here."*)

Employees feel safe challenging ideas and offering new

solutions.

• **Action Step:** Invite pushback. Say, *"Tell me what I might be missing."*

These four pillars create an environment where employees feel safe, valued, and engaged.

Practical Strategies to Build Trust & Psychological Safety

Strategy 1: Lead with Transparency

Share decisions, challenges, and rationale openly.
Example: "Here is why we are making this change and how it affects you."

Strategy 2: Show Vulnerability as a Leader

Admit mistakes to normalize learning culture.
Example: "I got this wrong. Here is how I'm adjusting."

Strategy 3: Encourage Questions & Feedback

Create a safe space for open conversations.
Example: "What is one thing I could do better as a leader?"

Strategy 4: Recognize & Reinforce Psychological Safety

Publicly acknowledge employees who take risks and challenge ideas.
Example: "I appreciate you speaking up. That is exactly

the kind of thinking we need."

Strategy 5: Set Boundaries That Protect Psychological Safety
Shut down blame, gossip, and fear-based behaviors.
Example: "Let's focus on solutions instead of pointing fingers."

The Impact of Psychological Safety on Performance

Research from Google's Project Aristotle found that psychological safety is the #1 predictor of high-performing teams. Teams that feel safe share ideas, solve problems faster, and collaborate more effectively.

Fact: A study by Harvard Business School found that hospitals where nurses felt safe reporting mistakes had fewer medical errors—because errors were fixed before they escalated.

Practical Application: 30-Day Trust-Building Challenge

For the next 30 days, implement one **trust-building strategy** each day.

Week 1: Build Inclusion Safety - Ask a team member for their perspective in a meeting.

Week 2: Strengthen Learner Safety - Share a mistake

you have learned from to normalize growth.

Week 3: Foster Contributor Safety - Delegate a key decision to an employee and empower them.

Week 4: Encourage Challenger Safety - Ask your team, "What is one assumption we should challenge?"

By the end of 30 days, your team culture will transform —creating a foundation of trust and psychological safety.

Key Takeaways

• Psychological safety and trust are the foundation of leadership success.

• High-trust cultures lead to engagement, innovation, and high performance.

• Leaders unknowingly erode trust through micromanagement, inconsistency, and unclear expectations.

• The four pillars of psychological safety create workplaces where people feel safe to contribute.

• Trust is built daily through transparency, vulnerability, and inclusive leadership.

What's Next?

Psychological safety sets the foundation for high-trust leadership, but what happens when leaders face resistance, uncertainty, and organizational change?

In the next chapter, we will explore how emotionally intelligent leaders navigate change, overcome resistance, and lead through uncertainty with confidence and clarity.

Great leadership is not just about making decisions— it's about guiding people through transformation.

Chapter 4:

Leading Through Change and Uncertainty with Emotional Intelligence

This chapter explores:

• Why change is difficult and how leaders can reduce resistance.

• The role of emotional intelligence (EQ) in navigating uncertainty.

• The difference between reactionary leadership and adaptive leadership.

• Practical strategies to lead teams through change with confidence and clarity.

• How to communicate change in a way that builds trust and commitment.

Why Change Triggers Resistance

*"It is not the strongest of the species that
survive, nor the most intelligent, but the one
most responsive to change." – Charles Darwin*

People don"t fear change itself; they fear the
uncertainty and potential loss that come with it.
Change disrupts routines, creates ambiguity, and
challenges established comfort zones.

When employees don't understand the reason
for change, they resist it. When they don't feel involved,
they disengage. Effective leaders can't eliminate
uncertainty, but they help people navigate it with
emotional intelligence, transparency, and trust.

The Psychology of Change: Why People Struggle with Uncertainty

Change is never just operational—it's deeply
psychological, and understanding why people struggle
with uncertainty is the key to leading them through it
with empathy and effectiveness.

• **Loss of Control:** People fear losing autonomy over
their roles or responsibilities.

• **Uncertainty and Ambiguity:** The unknown feels
threatening, triggering anxiety.

• **Comfort in Routine:** Change disrupts familiar

processes and expectations.

• **Fear of Failure:** People worry about adapting to new expectations or technologies.

• **Mistrust in Leadership:** If past changes were poorly handled, employees resist future changes.

Great leaders acknowledge these concerns instead of dismissing them. Instead of saying, "It's not a big deal," they say, "I know this change is hard. Let's talk about what's on your mind."

The Difference Between Reactive and Adaptive Leadership

Leaders who lack emotional intelligence often react to change instead of leading through it.

Reactive Leaders
• Resist or avoid change.
• Communicate reactively without a clear plan.
• Allow fear and uncertainty to drive decisions.
• Fail to involve employees in decision-making.
• Overpromise and underdeliver.

Adaptive Leaders
• Embrace change as an opportunity.
• Communicate proactively with clarity.
• Maintain emotional stability and confidence.
• Engage teams and gather input.
• Set realistic expectations and follow through.

Leaders with high emotional intelligence approach change with resilience, adaptability, and confidence— helping their teams do the same.

The Four Essential Actions of Leading Change

Action 1: Communicate the 'Why' Behind Change

Employees resist change when they do not understand its purpose. Leaders must clearly connect change to a larger mission.

• **Explain the why:** Frame change as a solution to a challenge or opportunity.
• **Make it personal:** Help employees see how it benefits them, not just the company.
• **Address concerns:** Acknowledge fears and provide transparency.

Instead of saying, "We are restructuring to optimize efficiency," say, "This change helps us work smarter, reduces unnecessary workload, and gives you more growth opportunities."

Action 2: Involve People in the Process

People support what they help create. The more employees feel heard and involved, the more they will embrace change.

• Gather feedback before finalizing changes.

• Assign team ambassadors to help roll out initiatives.
• Create open forums where employees can ask questions and share concerns.

Instead of making decisions in isolation, say: "Before we finalize this, I would love your input. What challenges do you foresee?"

Action 3: Provide Emotional Support and Stability
Uncertainty triggers stress. Leaders who stay calm, present, and supportive help employees feel grounded and confident.

• Acknowledge emotional reactions such as fear, frustration, and skepticism.
• Demonstrate emotional stability. Your team looks to you for cues.
• Offer reassurance and focus on what is not changing.

Instead of ignoring stress, say: "I know this transition is tough. What support would be most helpful right now?"

Action 4: Reinforce and Sustain the Change
Change is not a one-time announcement; it is a process. Leaders must reinforce the vision, track progress, and celebrate wins.

• Provide ongoing updates to maintain transparency.
• Recognize early adopters who embrace the change.
• Adjust based on feedback. Continuous learning

improves adoption.

Instead of assuming change will stick, say: "I would like to check in. How is this transition going for you? Any challenges?"

Communicating Change: Three Key Principles

Effective change leadership starts with how you communicate. These three principles ensure your message not only reaches people but also resonates, reduces resistance, and builds trust.

Principle 1: Clarity Over Complexity

Confusion creates resistance. Leaders must simplify their messaging to ensure everyone understands what is happening and why.

• Instead of saying: "Leadership has decided to implement new workflows to align with business objectives," say: "We are streamlining workflows to reduce unnecessary steps and free up more of your time for higher-impact work."

Principle 2: Repetition Over Assumption

Leaders assume that after one announcement, employees understand the change. They don't.

• Repeat key messages in meetings, emails, and one-on-one check-ins.
• Reinforce the change at multiple points until it

becomes the new norm.

Principle 3: Empathy Over Authority

Change communication should not feel top-down and transactional. It should be human-centered and reassuring.

• Instead of saying: "This is happening. Get ready," say: "I know this will take time to adjust to, and we will support you through it."

The Resilient Leader: Managing Your Own Emotions in Change

Leaders who manage their own stress and uncertainty are better equipped to help their teams adapt.

Practical Strategies for Leadership Resilience

• Pause before reacting. Take a breath and respond with intention.

• Reframe challenges as growth opportunities. Mindset shifts are powerful.

• Seek mentorship or peer support. You do not have to navigate change alone.

• Set boundaries. Avoid burnout by balancing strategy and self-care.

When leaders model calm, confident adaptability, teams follow suit.

Practical Application: The Change Readiness Challenge

For the next 30 days, apply one change leadership strategy daily:

Week 1: Clarify the Why - Ensure employees understand the purpose.

Week 2: Involve People - Gather input and empower early adopters.

Week 3: Communicate with Clarity and Empathy - Simplify messaging.

Week 4: Reinforce Change - Track progress and celebrate small wins.

By the end of the challenge, your team will embrace change more openly because they will feel supported, informed, and involved.

Key Takeaways

• Change triggers resistance when people feel uncertain or uninvolved.

• Reactive leaders fear change. Adaptive leaders guide people through it.

• Emotional intelligence is the key to leading change effectively.

• People support what they help create. Involve employees in decision-making.

• Clarity, repetition, and empathy make change easier to understand and embrace.

• Resilient leaders manage their own stress first, then support their teams.

What's Next?

Emotional intelligence is essential for leading through change, but what happens when change leads to conflict, tension, and misalignment within teams?

In the next chapter, we will explore how emotionally intelligent leaders manage conflict, turn tension into growth, and foster collaboration through effective communication and resolution strategies.

Great leadership is not just about managing change; it is about strengthening relationships in the process.

Chapter 5:

Conflict Resolution and Effective Communication

This chapter explores:

• The role of emotional intelligence in resolving workplace conflicts.

• Common sources of workplace conflict and how to address them.

• Communication techniques that de-escalate tensions and promote understanding.

• Structured conflict resolution models for leaders.

• How to handle difficult conversations with confidence and emotional intelligence.

The Role of Emotional Intelligence in Conflict Resolution

"The quality of our lives depends not on whether or not we have conflicts, but on how we respond to them." – Thomas Crum

Conflict is inevitable in leadership. Whether it arises from miscommunication, clashing personalities, or competing priorities, how a leader manages conflict determines whether it strengthens relationships or erodes trust.

When handled effectively, conflict:
• Fuels innovation by encouraging diverse perspectives.
• Encourages open dialogue that leads to better decision-making.
• Strengthens team collaboration by resolving misunderstandings.

When mishandled, it:
• Creates division and resentment within teams.
• Leads to disengagement and poor morale.
• Undermines trust and productivity.

Emotionally intelligent leaders:
• Stay calm under pressure and avoid reactive responses.

• Regulate emotional triggers to prevent impulsive decision-making.

• Practice active listening to fully understand different perspectives.

• Shift focus from blame to problem-solving and shared goals.

• Create a culture where disagreements are addressed constructively.

Understanding the Root Causes of Workplace Conflict

Conflict often does not stem from a single incident. Instead, underlying factors contribute to tension. Leaders must assess the root causes of conflict to resolve it effectively.

Common causes of conflict in the workplace:

• **Communication Breakdown** – Misunderstandings, lack of clarity, or poor information flow create confusion.

• **Unclear Expectations:** When roles, goals, or boundaries are ambiguous, misalignment occurs.

• **Personality Clashes:** Differences in work styles, values, or communication preferences lead to friction.

• **Power Struggles:** Competing priorities between teams, departments, or leadership levels cause tension.

• **Unresolved Past Issues:** Unaddressed disagreements

resurface and intensify over time.

Leaders can address the root causes of conflict by:
• Clarifying expectations early to prevent misunderstandings.

• Fostering open dialogue to encourage employees to voice concerns before they escalate.

• Encouraging perspective-taking to build empathy among team members.

• Modeling emotional regulation to create a culture of respect and constructive problem-solving.

Key Communication Strategies for Conflict Resolution

Conflict is inevitable in any workplace, but resolution depends on communication—these key strategies help leaders turn tension into productive dialogue, fostering understanding and collaboration.

Strategy 1: Active Listening (Understand Before Responding)

Many conflicts persist because people do not feel heard. Active listening ensures that all perspectives are acknowledged before attempting to resolve the issue.

• Give full attention to the speaker and avoid distractions.
• Pause before responding to fully process what is being said.

• Use verbal affirmations like "I see your point" or "That makes sense" to demonstrate understanding.
• Summarize what you heard to confirm clarity.

Example: Instead of saying: "I disagree, and here is why," say: "So what I am hearing is that you feel frustrated with the lack of clear direction. Is that correct?"

Strategy 2: Use "I" Statements Instead of "You" Accusations

Instead of saying: *"You never listen to me,"* which triggers defensiveness.

Say: "I feel unheard when I try to express my ideas." This reduces blame and keeps the conversation solution-focused.

Strategy 3: Regulate Tone and Body Language

Maintain an open posture (avoid crossing arms, which signals defensiveness).

• Speak with a steady, calm voice, even if tensions rise.
• Avoid aggressive language or sarcasm, which can worsen conflicts.

Strategy 4: Focus on Common Goals

• Shift from *who is right* to *what is best for the team or organization.*
• Reframe discussions to focus on shared goals and collaboration.

Conflict Resolution Models for Leaders

Different conflicts require different approaches. Below are three key conflict resolution models leaders can use.

1. The Thomas-Kilmann Conflict Mode Instrument

This model identifies *five conflict resolution styles*, each useful in different situations:

• **Competing:** Assertive and uncooperative; used when quick, decisive action is required.

• **Collaborating:** Assertive and cooperative; seeks win-win outcomes.

• **Compromising:** Middle ground; both parties give up something to reach an agreement.

• **Avoiding:** Used when the issue is trivial or needs time to cool down.

• **Accommodating:** Prioritizes relationships over personal interests.

2. The DESC Model: A Structured Way to Address Conflict

This four-step approach ensures direct yet respectful conflict resolution:

• **Describe:** Objectively state the issue.

• **Express:** Share emotions without blaming.

• **Specify:** Clarify the desired resolution.

• **Consequence:** Explain potential outcomes of action or inaction.

Example: Use the **DESC Approach**: "During the last meeting, I noticed that others did not have a chance to speak. I would like to ensure we all have time to share ideas. Moving forward, let's find ways to balance participation."

Instead of saying: "You always dominate meetings and don't let others contribute."

Navigating Difficult Conversations as a Leader

Difficult conversations, about performance, behavioral issues, or organizational changes, are challenging but necessary. Leaders who handle them with emotional intelligence strengthen trust and team cohesion.

Key Steps to Navigating Difficult Conversations
• **Prepare in Advance:** Clarify key points and anticipate emotional responses.

• **Set a Constructive Tone:** Express appreciation before delivering feedback.

• **Stick to Facts, Not Assumptions:** Focus on observable behavior rather than personal judgments.

• **Encourage Two-Way Dialogue:** Allow the other

person to share their perspective.

• **End with a Clear Path Forward:** Establish an action plan for resolution.

A Culture Where Conflict Leads to Growth

Strategies for Creating a Conflict-Positive Culture

• **Encourage Open Dialogue:** Normalize healthy disagreements as part of innovation and problem-solving.

• **Establish Conflict Resolution Norms:** Train employees in structured resolution techniques.

• **Recognize Constructive Conflict:** Reward teams who navigate disagreements effectively.

• **Hold Leaders Accountable:** Ensure that managers model emotionally intelligent conflict resolution.

Practical Application: The Conflict Resolution Challenge

For the next 30 days, practice resolving conflicts constructively:

Week 1: Actively listen and restate what you hear before responding.

Week 2: Use "I" statements instead of blame-focused language.

Week 3: Apply the DESC model in a difficult conversation.

Week 4: Encourage open feedback in team discussions.

By the end of the challenge, you'll have stronger conflict-resolution skills and a more collaborative team environment.

Key Takeaways

• Emotional intelligence is essential for effective conflict resolution.

• Active listening, tone regulation, and empathy prevent conflict escalation.

• Structured frameworks (TKI, DESC) provide clear resolution paths.

• Difficult conversations strengthen trust when handled with care.

• A conflict-positive culture fosters collaboration and innovation.

What's Next?

Now that we have explored conflict resolution and effective communication, the next chapter shifts focus to building a human-centered leadership culture.

We will examine the core principles of human-centered leadership and explore how leaders can foster psychologically safe workplaces where trust, empathy, and well-being drive team performance.

This chapter will also provide practical strategies for integrating human-centered leadership into daily practices, ensuring that leadership is not just about resolving conflicts but about creating an environment where people feel valued, engaged, and empowered to do their best work.

Chapter 6:

Building a Human-Centered Leadership Culture

This chapter explores:

• The principles of human-centered leadership.

• Why empathy, trust, and well-being are key to high-performing teams.

• How leaders can create a psychologically safe workplace.

• Practical strategies to integrate human-centered leadership into daily practices.

• The business case for human-centered leadership and its impact on organizational success.

What is Human-Centered Leadership?

*"Leadership is not about being in charge. It is
about taking care of those in your charge."*
– Simon Sinek

Leadership is often associated with strategy, execution,
and results. While these elements are critical,
leadership is fundamentally about people. **Human-
centered leadership prioritizes employees' well-being,
emotional health, and personal growth alongside
business objectives.**

A leader who fosters a human-first culture
creates an environment where employees feel valued,
engaged, and empowered to contribute their best
work. When employees thrive, so does the
organization.

Key Principles of Human-Centered Leadership

At its core, human-centered leadership is about putting
people first—creating workplaces where individuals
feel seen, heard, and valued. This approach isn't just
about being "nice"; it's about building the conditions
where people can do their best work. By leading with
empathy, fostering psychological safety, promoting
collaboration, supporting flexibility, and grounding
decisions in purpose, human-centered leaders create
cultures that drive both well-being and lasting success.

- **Empathy:** Understanding employees' emotions, perspectives, and experiences.

- **Psychological Safety:** Creating an environment where people feel safe to speak up.

- **Collaboration:** Encouraging teamwork, shared decision-making, and mutual respect.

- **Flexibility and Adaptability:** Supporting individual needs and work-life balance.

- **Purpose-Driven Leadership:** Aligning business goals with values that resonate with employees.

Why Human-Centered Leadership Matters

Research consistently shows that organizations with human-centered leadership experience:

- Higher employee engagement and retention.

- Increased creativity and innovation.

- Stronger collaboration and trust.

- Greater psychological safety, reducing workplace stress.

A study from *Google's Project Aristotle* found that the best-performing teams had one common factor—**psychological safety**. Employees who felt safe to express ideas and admit mistakes collaborated more effectively and took more creative risks.

When leaders prioritize people over rigid structures, they build teams that thrive and organizations that outperform competitors.

How Leaders Can Build a Human-Centered Workplace

A human-centered workplace doesn't emerge by chance—it's built through deliberate, ongoing actions that prioritize people at every level. Leaders play a critical role in shaping a culture where employees feel supported, valued, and psychologically safe, which fuels engagement, innovation, and long-term success. Building this kind of environment requires more than surface-level efforts; it means embedding empathy, trust, and inclusivity into everyday interactions and decision-making.

When leaders actively foster open communication, recognize contributions, support growth, and create space for diverse perspectives, they lay the foundation for a workplace where people—and the business—thrive.

1. Foster Open and Honest Communication
• Hold regular check-ins to discuss employee well-being and concerns.
• Encourage feedback without fear of repercussions.

- Model transparency in leadership decisions, sharing both successes and challenges.

2. Lead with Empathy and Emotional Intelligence
- Actively listen to employees and validate their experiences.
- Offer flexibility to accommodate personal and professional needs.
- Support employees during challenges, demonstrating genuine care.

3. Recognize and Celebrate Contributions
- Create peer-to-peer recognition programs that allow employees to appreciate each other's efforts.
- Replace outdated performance reviews with real-time feedback and coaching.
- Celebrate small and big wins in team meetings to reinforce a culture of appreciation.

4. Create Opportunities for Growth and Development
- Invest in mentorship programs to help employees build new skills.
- Offer professional development opportunities, such as training, workshops, and coaching.
- Empower employees with leadership opportunities and decision-making responsibilities.

5. Promote Psychological Safety and Inclusivity

• Ensure all voices are valued, regardless of position or background.

• Address and eliminate biases that may create barriers to inclusion.

• Create safe spaces for discussions on diversity, equity, and mental health.

Case Study: How Indra Nooyi Transformed PepsiCo's Culture

As CEO of PepsiCo, *Indra Nooyi* was known for her human-centered leadership approach. She believed that leaders should deeply understand their employees' experiences and make decisions that support both business success and personal well-being.

Key Actions That Drove Cultural Transformation

• **Personalized Leadership:** She wrote personal letters to employees' families, acknowledging their contributions.

• **Well-Being Initiatives:** Introduced policies that supported work-life balance and holistic wellness.

• **Diversity and Inclusion:** Pioneered programs that promoted women and underrepresented employees into leadership.

Outcome: Under Nooyi's leadership, *PepsiCo became known for its people-first culture*, resulting in higher employee engagement, increased innovation, and long-term business success.

The Business Case for Human-Centered Leadership

Some leaders resist prioritizing people over processes, fearing it will compromise efficiency or profitability. However, research shows that human-centered leadership drives business success.

Key Business Benefits

• **Higher Retention Rates:** Employees who feel valued stay longer, reducing hiring and training costs.

• **Improved Productivity:** Engaged employees contribute more effectively.

• **Stronger Brand Reputation:** Companies known for strong workplace culture attract top talent.

• **Increased Customer Satisfaction:** Employees who feel supported provide better service and innovation.

Companies like *Microsoft, Google, and Salesforce* have all integrated human-centered leadership into their business strategies, leading to record-breaking innovation, employee satisfaction, and financial performance.

Practical Steps to Implement Human-Centered Leadership

Step 1: Self-Assessment

• Reflect on leadership practices – Are decisions aligned with employee well-being?

• Gather anonymous feedback from employees on workplace culture.

Step 2: Set Clear People-First Goals

• Identify key areas where employee experience can improve.

• Set measurable objectives, such as reducing burnout or increasing employee engagement.

Step 3: Implement Systemic Changes

• Introduce flexible work policies.

• Provide mental health resources.

• Encourage open discussions on psychological safety.

Step 4: Lead by Example

• Model vulnerability and transparency.

• Show employees that leadership is committed to a human-centered culture.

The Future of Leadership: Why Human-Centered Approaches Matter More Than Ever

As organizations face rapid change, AI-driven

automation, and workforce shifts, the need for humanized leadership is stronger than ever. While AI can optimize efficiency, **it cannot replace the need for human connection, trust, and psychological safety.**

Human-Centered Leadership in the AI Era
• AI will automate tasks, but leaders must strengthen emotional intelligence.

• Employees will demand purpose-driven workplaces where they feel valued.

• Organizations that invest in human potential will attract and retain top talent.

Leaders who embrace a **human-centered approach** will create the workplaces of the future—where innovation thrives, employees flourish, and organizations succeed sustainably.

Key Takeaways
• Human-centered leadership prioritizes people as the foundation of organizational success.

• Psychological safety, trust, and empathy drive engagement and innovation.

• Leaders can foster a people-first culture by integrating open communication, recognition, and well-being initiatives.

• Research confirms that human-centered leadership improves retention, productivity, and financial performance.

• In the AI era, human connection is more critical than ever for workplace success.

What's Next?

Now that we have explored how human-centered leadership creates thriving workplaces, the next chapter will focus on the power of authenticity and ethical leadership, examining why authenticity is essential for effective leadership and how ethical decision-making fosters trust and long-term success. We'll also explore strategies for aligning leadership actions with core values, providing practical frameworks to navigate ethical challenges with integrity, helping leaders build credibility, strengthen workplace culture, and drive lasting change.

Chapter 7:

Leading with Authenticity and Ethical Leadership

This chapter explores:

• Why authenticity is essential for modern leadership.

• How ethical leadership fosters trust and long-term success.

• The role of vulnerability and transparency in building credibility.

• Strategies for aligning leadership actions with core values.

• Practical frameworks for ethical decision-making.

The Importance of Authenticity in Leadership

"Authenticity is the alignment of head, mouth, heart, and feet— thinking, saying, feeling, and doing the same thing—consistently. This builds trust, and followers love leaders they can trust." – Lance Secretan

In an era of growing skepticism toward leadership, authenticity has become a critical differentiator between **leaders who inspire and those who merely manage.** Employees and stakeholders want to work with leaders who are **genuine, transparent, and aligned with their values.**

Why Authenticity Matters

Research shows that employees working under **authentic leaders** are more engaged, innovative, and committed to their organization.

Authentic leadership:

• **Builds trust**, making employees feel safe and valued.

• **Enhances engagement**, fostering deeper team commitment.

• **Encourages psychological safety**, allowing employees to express ideas and concerns.

• **Strengthens decision-making** by ensuring

consistency and integrity.

Authenticity does not mean perfection—it means
consistency. Employees respect leaders who are
honest about challenges, take responsibility for their
actions, and stay true to their values.

Signs of Authentic Leadership
• Actions align with stated values and beliefs.

• Communication is transparent, even when delivering
difficult news.

• Vulnerability is embraced but balanced with strength.

• Decisions are made with **integrity, not just short-
term gain.**

How Leaders Can Cultivate Authenticity
Authentic leadership isn't about playing a role—it's
about leading with clarity, consistency, and integrity in
a way that builds lasting trust. To cultivate authenticity,
leaders must balance vulnerability with authority, stay
grounded in their core values, and make ethical
decisions that reflect both personal and organizational
responsibility.

1. The Three C's of Authentic Leadership
• **Clarity:** Define and communicate your core values so
your team understands what drives your decisions.
• **Consistency:** Align your actions with your principles

to reinforce credibility and trust.

• **Confidence:** Be open about challenges while maintaining strategic focus and decisiveness.

2. Balancing Vulnerability and Authority

Authenticity does not mean oversharing personal struggles or appearing uncertain. **Leaders must strike a balance** between being relatable and maintaining authority.

• **Be open but maintain professionalism:** Share lessons learned from challenges rather than unfiltered emotions.

• **Lead with confidence while inviting input:** Acknowledge when you do not have all the answers, but trust your team to find solutions together.

• **Ensure words and actions align:** Employees notice inconsistencies, which can quickly erode trust.

3. Ethical Leadership and Decision-Making

Ethical leadership is about more than compliance; it involves making decisions that reflect fairness, integrity, and social responsibility. Ethical leaders prioritize doing what is right, even when it is difficult or unpopular.

Key Principles of Ethical Leadership

• **Fairness:** Treat all employees and stakeholders with equity and impartiality.

• **Transparency:** Communicate openly about decisions,

processes, and challenges.

• **Accountability:** Take responsibility for actions and decisions, acknowledging mistakes and learning from them.

• **Long-Term Thinking:** Consider the broader impact of decisions on employees, customers, and communities.

Ethical leaders do not just follow rules, they create cultures of honesty, integrity, and responsibility.

Using The Ethical Lens Framework for Decision-Making

When faced with ethical dilemmas, leaders should assess the situation through multiple perspectives:

• **Rights-Based Lens:** Is this decision fair and just for all stakeholders?

• **Results-Based Lens:** What are the short-term vs. long-term consequences?

• **Relationship-Based Lens:** Does this decision strengthen or weaken trust?

• **Reputation-Based Lens:** Would I be comfortable if this decision were made public?

Example: Unilever's sustainability initiatives have proven that profitability and ethical leadership can coexist. By prioritizing ethical business practices, the company strengthened brand loyalty and investor confidence.

Case Study: Nelson Mandela's Leadership of Integrity

Few leaders embody authenticity and ethical leadership as profoundly as Nelson Mandela. His leadership was rooted in deep personal integrity, resilience, and an unwavering commitment to justice.

Key Leadership Actions That Defined Mandela's Legacy
• **Unwavering Commitment to Values:** Even after 27 years in prison, Mandela refused to abandon his principles of justice, equality, and reconciliation.

• **Ethical Decision-Making:** Instead of seeking revenge, he prioritized unity and healing, demonstrating moral courage over personal or political gain.

• **Leading with Transparency:** He openly communicated his vision for a peaceful, democratic South Africa, ensuring people understood the purpose behind his leadership.

Outcome: Mandela's **authenticity and ethical leadership** not only helped dismantle apartheid but also transformed a nation, proving that integrity and compassion are powerful leadership tools.

Fostering an Ethical and Inclusive Workplace

Inclusive leaders recognize the emotional impact of exclusion and actively **work to create a culture where all employees feel valued and respected**. Ethical leadership extends beyond internal policies—it involves making a meaningful impact on society.

How to Foster an Inclusive Workplace

• **Promote equitable hiring and advancement practices:** Ensure equal opportunities for all employees.

• **Encourage diverse perspectives**: Create spaces where employees from different backgrounds feel empowered to share insights.

• **Address unconscious bias:** Provide training and awareness programs to help employees recognize and challenge biases.

• **Commit to social responsibility:** Engage in corporate social responsibility (CSR) initiatives that align with company values and contribute to community well-being.

Example: Companies like Patagonia have built their reputations on corporate social responsibility by ensuring ethical supply chains, reducing environmental impact, and investing in community development.

The Business Case for Ethical Leadership

Some leaders may believe ethical leadership slows

down decision-making or interferes with profitability. However, organizations that prioritize ethics experience greater long-term success.

Key Business Benefits of Ethical Leadership
• **Higher Employee Retention:** People stay in workplaces where they feel respected and valued.

• **Increased Customer Loyalty:** Consumers support brands that align with their values.

• **Stronger Brand Reputation:** Ethical businesses attract investors and partners who prioritize sustainability.

• **Reduced Legal and Compliance Risks:** Ethical leaders proactively prevent workplace misconduct.

When leaders prioritize ethics, they reduce organizational risk, build stronger relationships, and ensure sustainable success.

Final Thoughts: The Path to Ethical and Authentic Leadership

Authentic and ethical leadership is not about perfection, it is about consistency, transparency, and alignment with values. Leaders who prioritize authenticity build stronger relationships, foster inclusive workplaces, and make ethical decisions that contribute to long-term success.

Leadership Challenge for the Week

• **Reflect**: What is one personal value that defines your leadership style?

• **Assess**: Are your decisions and leadership behaviors consistently aligned with this value?

• **Act**: Ask your team for anonymous feedback on how authentic and ethical your leadership feels—use insights to strengthen trust and engagement.

Key Takeaways

• Authenticity is a key leadership trait that builds trust and engagement.

• Ethical leadership involves fairness, transparency, accountability, and long-term thinking.

• The Ethical Lens Framework helps leaders navigate complex decision-making.

• Diversity, inclusion, and social responsibility are essential components of ethical leadership.

• Organizations that prioritize ethics experience stronger financial performance and employee loyalty.

What's Next?

As we approach the final chapters, we will explore how

to apply emotional intelligence in daily leadership practice. Leading with authenticity and ethics creates the foundation for success, but true leadership growth comes from continuous reflection, learning, and action.

The next chapter provides a practical roadmap for integrating emotional intelligence into your leadership journey. Let's explore how to turn these insights into daily leadership habits that drive long-term success.

Chapter 8:

The Path to Emotionally Intelligent Leadership

This chapter explores:

• How emotional intelligence becomes a lifelong leadership practice.

• Practical strategies to integrate emotional intelligence into daily leadership.

• The role of continuous learning and self-reflection in leadership growth.

• How emotionally intelligent leaders navigate challenges, uncertainty, and transformation.

The Journey Toward Emotionally Intelligent Leadership

"Before you are a leader, success is all about growing yourself. When you become a leader, success is all about growing others." – Jack Welch

Emotional intelligence is not just a leadership skill—it is a lifelong commitment to self-awareness, continuous growth, and human connection. The best leaders are not those who claim to have all the answers but those who consistently learn, adapt, and refine their leadership approach.

Leadership does not exist in isolation. It influences teams, organizational culture, and the well-being of individuals. Leaders who prioritize emotional intelligence create work environments where trust, collaboration, and innovation thrive. More importantly, they leave a lasting impact on the people they lead, shaping organizations that are resilient, adaptable, and deeply human-centered.

As AI continues to automate tasks and decision-making, the need for emotionally intelligent leadership becomes more urgent than ever. Technology can optimize processes, but it cannot replace human connection, trust, and the ability to inspire. The future of leadership belongs to those who embrace both technological advancements and the deeply human elements of leadership.

Key Lessons from Emotionally Intelligent Leaders

Throughout this book, we have explored how emotional intelligence transforms leadership. From Nelson Mandela's integrity to Satya Nadella's empathy-driven transformation of Microsoft, emotionally intelligent leaders share common traits that contribute to their effectiveness.

Common Traits of Emotionally Intelligent Leaders
• **Self-Awareness:** They recognize their strengths, limitations, and emotional triggers.

• **Empathy:** They understand and validate the experiences of others.

• **Resilience:** They manage stress, navigate uncertainty, and model emotional regulation.

• **Authenticity:** They lead with integrity and transparency.

• **Ethical Decision-Making:** They prioritize fairness, accountability, and long-term impact.

• **Commitment to Growth:** They continuously seek improvement and feedback.

These traits are not inherent personality traits, but they can be developed, refined, and strengthened over time.

Building Your Own Leadership Development Plan

Leadership growth does not happen by accident. It requires *self-reflection, goal setting, and continuous learning.* Use the following framework to create a *personalized leadership development plan* focused on emotional intelligence.

Step 1: Assess Your Current Emotional Intelligence

*Start with honest **self-reflection** or formal assessments. Consider using:*

1. 360-Degree Feedback: Ask peers, employees, and mentors for input on your leadership style.

2. Journaling: Reflect on emotional triggers, leadership successes, and challenges.

3. EQ Assessments: Use validated emotional intelligence assessments to identify strengths and areas for growth.

Questions for Reflection

• How do I typically respond to stress or conflict?
• Do I create an environment where employees feel psychologically safe?
• How often do I practice active listening and empathy in conversations?
• Do my leadership actions align with my values?

Step 2: Set Leadership Development Goals

Based on your assessment, set clear, **actionable goals** for improvement. Goals should be **specific, measurable, and aligned with your leadership vision.**

Examples of Emotional Intelligence Development Goals
1. Improve Active Listening: Dedicate time in each meeting to listening without interrupting.

2. Enhance Self-Regulation: Implement mindfulness techniques to manage stress and maintain composure under pressure.

3. Increase Empathetic Leadership: Schedule regular one-on-one check-ins with employees to understand their challenges.

4. Strengthen Conflict Resolution Skills: Use structured conflict resolution frameworks when addressing disagreements.

Step 3: Implement Daily Leadership Practices
Emotional intelligence is built through consistent, intentional practice. Small daily actions lead to significant leadership transformation over time.

1. Self-Awareness Practices
• Keep a leadership journal to track emotions and decision-making patterns.
• Ask for feedback from a trusted mentor or peer.

2. Emotional Regulation Techniques

• Use deep breathing exercises before responding to high-pressure situations.

• Reframe challenges as learning opportunities instead of obstacles.

3. Empathy and Active Listening Strategies

Dedicate time in meetings to truly hear employee concerns.

Validate emotions before offering solutions.

4. Trust and Psychological Safety Building

• Encourage honest conversations without fear of judgment.

• Acknowledge your own mistakes to normalize learning from failure.

5. Ethical Decision-Making

• Pause before making major decisions to consider long-term impact.

• Use the Ethical Lens Framework to weigh fairness, relationships, and reputation.

The Future of Emotionally Intelligent Leadership

The workplace is evolving. Rapid technological advancements, AI-driven automation, and shifting employee expectations require leaders to adapt in new ways. Emotional intelligence will become even more critical as organizations prioritize mental well-being, ethical leadership, and inclusive cultures.

Trends Shaping the Future of Leadership
• **Human-Centered Workplaces:** Organizations will continue to prioritize employee well-being, engagement, and flexibility.

• **AI and Emotional Intelligence:** As AI automates tasks, emotional intelligence will remain a key differentiator in leadership.

• **Inclusive Leadership:** Leaders will need to cultivate empathy and cultural intelligence to foster diverse, equitable work environments.

• **Resilience in Uncertain Times:** Navigating economic shifts, global crises, and industry disruptions will require emotionally intelligent leadership.

While AI can analyze data and optimize efficiency, only human leaders can inspire, connect, and lead with emotional intelligence.

Taking the Next Step: Applying Emotional Intelligence Daily

The most successful leaders are those who commit to growth, reflection, and action. Emotionally intelligent leadership is not about a single moment of insight—it is about continuous learning and intentional practice.

Final Leadership Challenge

• **Reflect on Your Growth:** Identify **three key insights** from this book that you will implement in your leadership.

• **Commit to One Daily Practice:** Choose a strategy from this book and apply it consistently over the next **30 days**.

• **Seek Feedback:** Ask a trusted colleague or mentor to assess your **emotional intelligence progress**.

• **Share Your Learning:** Teach a leadership team member or peer about an **EQ concept** to reinforce your understanding.

Embracing **emotional intelligence is a lifelong journey**. The more you invest in understanding yourself and others, the more you will *inspire trust, resilience, and excellence in those around you.*

Key Takeaways

• Emotional intelligence is a continuous leadership practice, not a fixed trait.

• Self-reflection and structured leadership development plans drive growth.

• Daily leadership practices enhance emotional intelligence over time.

- The future of leadership will require both AI and human-centered emotional intelligence.

- Emotionally intelligent leadership fosters resilience, trust, and adaptability.

What's Next?

As we approach the conclusion of this book, we shift from theory to action. Leadership is not just about knowing, it is about doing.

The final chapter will focus on applying emotional intelligence beyond the workplace, exploring how it shapes personal relationships, mentorship, social impact, and lifelong leadership growth.

The best leaders do not stop learning, they apply their knowledge every day to transform their teams, organizations, and communities.

Chapter 9:

The Future of Human-Centered Leadership

This chapter explores:

• The evolution of leadership and why emotional intelligence remains a critical skill.

• The role of human-centered leadership in a world increasingly shaped by AI and automation.

• How leaders can future-proof their leadership by balancing technological advancements with emotional intelligence.

• Practical strategies to sustain personal growth and leadership impact in an ever-changing world.

The Evolution of Leadership: Why Human-Centered Leadership Matters More Than Ever

"The best way to predict the future is to create it."
— Peter Drucker

Leadership has never been static. It has evolved across generations, industries, and organizational structures. Yet, while the tools and contexts of leadership may shift, one truth remains constant—leadership is fundamentally about people.

In an era where AI, automation, and digital transformation are reshaping the way we work, some wonder if the need for human-centered leadership will diminish. The reality? Emotional intelligence, adaptability, and trust-building are more critical than ever.

The Leadership Evolution Model: From Authority to Human-Centered Visionary

Leadership is not static—it evolves alongside the changing needs of people, organizations, and society. The Leadership Evolution Model traces this shift from traditional authority-driven leadership to a future led by human-centered visionaries who blend emotional intelligence, strategic foresight, and adaptability to meet the challenges of a rapidly transforming world.

1. The Command-and-Control Era (20th Century Leadership)

Leadership was defined by hierarchy, authority, and rigid structures.

Success was measured by efficiency and output, not by engagement or culture.

2. The Servant Leadership & Emotional Intelligence Era (Late 20th - Early 21st Century Leadership)

Leadership shifted towards people-first approaches, recognizing that engaged teams drive better results.

Emotional intelligence (EQ) emerged as a key driver of effective leadership.

3. The Human-Centered Visionary Era (Present & Future Leadership)

The modern leader must integrate emotional intelligence, strategic vision, and adaptability.

AI and automation optimize processes, but leaders who connect, inspire, and engage will create the most enduring impact.

The Future Belongs to Leaders Who Can Bridge Technology and Human Connection

While AI can analyze data, predict trends, and streamline decision-making, it **cannot replicate**:

• **Trust and Psychological Safety** – Teams follow leaders who create environments where people feel valued and safe to innovate.

• **Vision and Inspiration** – AI can optimize efficiency, but it cannot motivate people toward a shared purpose.

• **Ethical Judgment** – Leadership requires the ability to balance long-term impact, fairness, and human dignity.

• **Adaptability and Emotional Intelligence** – The ability to read emotional cues, resolve conflict, and foster collaboration remains a defining leadership skill.

The leaders of the future will embrace technology while remaining deeply human-centered.

The Human-Centered Leadership Model for the Future

To thrive in the future of work, leaders must develop three core capabilities:

1. Attuned Leadership: Emotional Intelligence in the Age of AI

• Recognizing when to lead with human connection vs. when to leverage AI-driven insights.

• Practicing deep listening and reading emotional cues, even in digital communication.

• Creating emotionally intelligent hybrid workplaces that blend remote, in-person, and AI-assisted collaboration.

Practical Strategies

- Incorporate AI-powered feedback tools, but supplement them with real, human dialogue.
- Use virtual reality (VR) empathy training to enhance leadership EQ in digital spaces.
- Ensure that workplace automation enhances, rather than replaces, human engagement.

2. Adaptive Leadership: Thriving in Uncertainty and Complexity

- Leading through disruptive change and market shifts with confidence.
- Using emotional resilience and adaptability to navigate crises and uncertainty.
- Encouraging a learning culture that embraces curiosity, agility, and experimentation.

Practical Strategies

- Train teams in adaptive thinking and problem-solving through scenario-based simulations.
- Develop a personal resilience toolkit that includes mindfulness, self-reflection, and cognitive flexibility.
- Emphasize growth mindset leadership, encouraging learning and innovation from failures.

3. Ethical and Visionary Leadership: Leading with Purpose

- Balancing profitability with ethical responsibility in decision-making.

- Designing workplace cultures that foster inclusion, psychological safety, and long-term impact.
- Leading with clarity of purpose, ensuring that mission, values, and leadership actions align.

Practical Strategies
- Create a Leadership Vision Statement, revisiting it regularly to ensure alignment.
- Implement AI-ethics decision frameworks to assess the social and human impact of leadership decisions.
- Embed psychological safety principles into company structures to ensure inclusive and ethical leadership.

Sustaining Growth as a Human-Centered Leader

Leadership is not a one-time achievement—it is a lifelong journey. To remain relevant, effective, and impactful, leaders must commit to continuous self-improvement.

Personal Growth Plan for Future-Ready Leaders

1. Emotional Resilience and Well-Being
- Dedicate time to self-reflection, journaling, and leadership evaluation.

- Engage in continuous education, staying ahead of industry trends, leadership innovations, and personal development practices.

- Seek mentorship and coaching to challenge perspectives and enhance decision-making.

2. Emotional Resilience and Well-Being

• Build routines that prioritize mental and emotional health to sustain leadership effectiveness.

• Develop self-regulation strategies, ensuring you remain calm and clear-headed in high-pressure situations.

• Encourage work-life integration, recognizing that well-being fuels long-term leadership impact.

3. Creating a Lasting Leadership Legacy

• Actively mentor and develop future leaders, sharing insights and creating a ripple effect of positive impact.

• Lead in a way that aligns with personal values and organizational mission, leaving behind a culture of excellence, inclusion, and innovation.

• Focus on long-term influence, ensuring leadership decisions have enduring positive effects on teams, industries, and society.

Key Takeaways

• Leadership is evolving, but emotional intelligence and human connection remain critical.

• AI and automation will enhance leadership, but cannot replace trust, vision, and ethical judgment.

• Future-ready leaders must integrate emotional

intelligence, adaptability, and ethical leadership.

• Sustained leadership impact requires ongoing learning, resilience, and mentorship.

• Leaders must build a legacy that prioritizes both people and progress.

What's Next?

This chapter marks the culmination of this book, but not the end of the leadership journey.

The next and final chapter will bring everything together, offering a roadmap for implementing the principles of human-centered leadership into daily practice.

Leadership is not about having all the answers—it is about having the courage, adaptability, and emotional intelligence to inspire transformation in people, organizations, and society.

Chapter 10:

Bringing It All Together – Your Human Centered Leadership Road Map

This chapter explores:

• A structured framework for integrating emotional intelligence into daily leadership.

• How to sustain human-centered leadership in a rapidly evolving world.

• A step-by-step action plan to implement the key principles from this book.

• Reflection questions to help leaders personalize their leadership growth journey.

The Human-Centered Leadership Framework: A Recap

*"A journey of a thousand miles begins with
a single step." – Lao Tzu*

Throughout this book, we have explored the essential
components of human-centered leadership—how
emotional intelligence, psychological safety, resilience,
and ethical leadership create lasting impact.

This final chapter provides a practical roadmap
for leaders to apply these concepts in a structured,
intentional way.

The Core Pillars of Human-Centered Leadership

To put human-centered leadership into action, it helps
to anchor your approach in a clear set of guiding
principles, these core pillars serve as the foundation for
leading with empathy, integrity, and lasting impact:

• **Emotional Intelligence:** The ability to understand and
manage emotions, both in yourself and others.

• **Psychological Safety:** Creating an environment
where people feel safe to express ideas, take risks, and
grow.

• **Resilience & Adaptability:** Staying steady in
uncertainty, leading through change, and fostering

team resilience.

• **Ethical Leadership:** Making values-driven decisions that prioritize integrity, trust, and long-term success.

• **Transformational Influence:** Inspiring, motivating, and engaging others through clear vision and authentic leadership.

The Human-Centered Leadership Roadmap

Transforming leadership habits takes intentional practice. Below is a **five-step roadmap** to guide your implementation of **human-centered leadership** principles.

Step 1: Assess Where You Are Today

Before making changes, take stock of your current leadership style.

Self-Assessment Questions

• How self-aware am I in high-pressure situations?
• Do I regularly seek feedback from my team on my leadership style?
• How well do I foster psychological safety within my team?
• Do I adapt well to change, or do I struggle with uncertainty?
• How effectively do I inspire and engage my team?

Action

▶ Conduct a 360-degree feedback assessment. Ask colleagues, employees, and mentors for insights into your strengths and areas for improvement.

▶ Reflect on past leadership decisions. Where did you lead with emotional intelligence, and where could you improve?

Step 2: Set Intentional Leadership Goals

Great leaders do not just react, they *set intentional goals* to refine their leadership approach.

SMART Goal-Setting Framework for Leadership

• **Specific:** Clearly define the leadership behavior or skill you want to develop.

• **Measurable:** Identify key indicators of progress.

• **Achievable:** Set realistic, actionable goals.

• **Relevant:** Align goals with your leadership role and team needs.

• **Time-bound:** Set a time frame to track progress.

Example Leadership Goals

• **Enhancing Emotional Intelligence:** "For the next three months, I will practice active listening by summarizing key points in conversations before responding."

• **Building Psychological Safety:** "I will implement a 'no-blame' culture by regularly reframing mistakes as learning opportunities in team meetings."

• **Strengthening Resilience:** "I will use mindfulness techniques to regulate stress and avoid reactive decision-making."

Step 3: Develop Daily Leadership Practices
Leadership is built in small, consistent actions.

Human-Centered Leadership Daily Practices
• **Morning Reflection:** Set an intention for the day: "How will I lead with emotional intelligence today?"

• **Active Listening Challenge:** Focus fully on one conversation daily without distractions.

• **Psychological Safety Check:** At the end of meetings, ask: "Did everyone feel heard? What could we improve?"

• **Leadership Self-Regulation Exercise:** When feeling stressed, pause and take a deep breath before responding.

• **Recognition Ritual:** Each week, acknowledge and appreciate team members' efforts in a personalized way.

Action
► Select two to three daily leadership habits to implement for the next 30 days.
► Keep a journal to track progress and reflect on leadership wins and challenges.

Step 4: Foster a Human-Centered Leadership Culture
To truly transform an organization, human-centered leadership must extend beyond individual practices and shape team culture.

Key Culture-Shaping Strategies
• **Normalize Feedback:** Create a continuous feedback culture where people feel comfortable giving and receiving input.

• **Encourage Psychological Safety:** Lead by example—admit mistakes, ask for feedback, and embrace diverse perspectives.

• **Promote Well-Being:** Implement policies that prioritize mental health, such as flexible work arrangements or wellness initiatives.

• **Support Growth & Development:** Provide mentorship, training, and opportunities for employees to lead projects.

Action
► Identify one major cultural shift you want to champion in your organization.
► Share your leadership journey with your team, encouraging them to join in creating a human-centered workplace.

Step 5: Evaluate Progress and Adapt
Sustaining leadership growth requires continuous

learning, reflection, and adaptation.

Leadership Reflection Questions
• How have I grown as a leader in the past six months?
• Where have I seen positive changes in my team's engagement and trust?
• What leadership challenges am I still navigating?
• What additional support, mentorship, or resources do I need?

Action
▶ Schedule a quarterly leadership review to assess progress on your leadership goals.
▶ Adjust strategies based on feedback, team needs, and evolving organizational dynamics.

The Human-Centered Leadership Challenge

Over the next **90 days**, commit to implementing at least **one principle** from each leadership pillar.

Challenge Checklist
▶ **Emotional Intelligence:** Practice self-awareness by identifying emotional triggers in leadership situations.

▶ **Psychological Safety:** Encourage open dialogue and ensure team members feel heard.

▶ **Resilience & Adaptability:** Model calm, solution-focused leadership in moments of uncertainty.

► **Ethical Leadership:** Make at least one leadership decision that prioritizes long-term integrity over short-term gain.

► **Transformational Influence:** Deliver a clear, inspiring message about the team's shared purpose.

Final Thought: Leadership is a journey, not a destination. Every small action you take strengthens your ability to lead with impact, influence, and integrity.

Key Takeaways

• Leadership transformation happens through daily intentional actions.

• Assess your current leadership style to identify growth areas.

• Set SMART leadership goals to guide progress.

• Develop small daily habits that reinforce emotional intelligence and human-centered leadership.

• Shape team culture by normalizing psychological safety and trust.

• Commit to continuous growth, reflection, and adaptability.

What's Next?

This book has provided a roadmap for embracing emotional intelligence and human-centered leadership. But leadership growth does not stop here.

The next step? Exploring how transformational leadership takes human-centered leadership to the next level.

Conclusion:
The Future of Human-Centered Leadership

This chapter explores:

• The lasting impact of human-centered leadership in a changing world.

• The integration of emotional intelligence, mental health, and transformational leadership.

• How to sustain leadership growth beyond this book.

• A preview of the next stage in the leadership journey.

The Future of Leadership
is Human-Centered

*"You are never 'done.' You are simply at another
level of your journey."* – Unknown

Leadership is evolving. The world is more complex,
diverse, and fast-paced than ever before. Organizations
are no longer looking for authoritative managers—they
need emotionally intelligent, adaptable, and human-
centered leaders who inspire, engage, and elevate
those around them.

As artificial intelligence and automation
continue to reshape industries, the most valuable
leadership skills will not be technical—they will be
human. Leaders who master emotional intelligence,
psychological safety, and transformational influence
will define the future of leadership.

This book has explored the power of emotional
intelligence and mental health in leadership. The key
takeaway? Your greatest leadership superpower is not
just what you know—it's how you connect, inspire, and
support others.

Sustaining Your Human-Centered Leadership Journey

Great leadership isn't a destination—it's a lifelong
journey of growth, self-awareness, and impact. The

best leaders don't stop learning. They continuously refine their ability to lead with purpose, integrity, and resilience.

Five Ways to Continue Your Leadership Growth

1. Commit to Lifelong Learning

Read books, listen to podcasts, and attend leadership development programs.
Stay informed about new research on emotional intelligence and workplace well-being.

2. Seek Feedback Regularly

• Ask your team: *How am I doing as a leader? Where can I improve?*
• Create a culture where honest feedback is welcomed and valued.

3. Develop the Next Generation of Leaders

• Mentor emerging leaders by sharing your insights and experiences.
• Create opportunities for your team members to take on leadership roles.

4. Adapt to Change with Resilience

• Stay flexible in the face of uncertainty and model composure under pressure.
• Approach leadership challenges with a **learning mindset** instead of fear.

5. Prioritize Self-Care and Mental Health

• Burnout is real even for the best leaders. Take care of your well-being so you can show up as your best self.
• Encourage mental health initiatives within your organization to create a thriving workplace culture.

Leadership is an Invitation

Great leadership is **not about power or control;** it is about creating an environment where people **thrive, innovate, and contribute at their highest potential.**

Leadership is an **invitation...**

- • An invitation to **show up, engage, and inspire.**

- • An invitation to **lead with courage, integrity, and authenticity.**

- • An invitation to **make an impact that lasts far beyond you.**

The world does not need more leaders who manage. **It needs more leaders who elevate...**and that starts with you.

Preview of Next Book

The Human-Centered Leader: The First Power of Transformational Leadership

Introduction: The First Power of Transformational Leadership

In *Leadership is Human*, we explored emotional intelligence as the foundation of human-centered leadership. Now, it's time to take the next step.

The book, **The Human-Centered Leader: The First Power of Transformational Leadership**, focuses on how emotionally intelligent leaders move from connection to influence, shaping cultures of innovation, engagement, and high performance.

Leadership is not just about managing teams— it's about transforming them. Leaders who master *The First Power of Transformational Leadership* create movements, not just management strategies.

The First Power of Transformational Leadership: Human-Centered Influence

Influence—not authority—is the currency of transformational leadership.

What Separates Transformational Leaders from Traditional Leaders?

• Traditional leaders command compliance.

- Transformational leaders inspire commitment.
- Traditional leaders prioritize efficiency.
- Transformational leaders cultivate engagement.
- Traditional leaders rely on structure.
- Transformational leaders build culture.

In this book, we will explore how to master transformational influence, moving from transactional leadership to high-impact, human-centered transformation.

What You'll Learn in This Book

This book is your guide to mastering the human side of leadership—where influence, trust, and vision come together to create lasting impact and transformational change.

- The science of influence and motivation in leadership

- How to inspire lasting commitment, not just compliance

- The three superpowers of transformational leadership

- How to build a culture of trust, vision, and communication

- Real-world case studies of leaders who create movements

The Three Superpowers of Transformational Leadership

To unlock the full potential of human-centered leadership, three transformational superpowers equip leaders to meet the demands of a rapidly evolving world while creating lasting impact.

Power 1: The Attuned Leader – Mastering deep human connection and emotional insight.

Power 2: The Psychologically Agile Leader – Adapting, thriving, and leading in uncertainty.

Power 3: The Emotionally Intelligent Strategist – Balancing influence, vision, and execution.

Each superpower builds on the *Leadership is Human* framework, turning emotional intelligence into action that transforms teams, organizations, and industries.

The Next Level of Leadership Mastery

If *Leadership is Human* was about laying the foundation, *The Human-Centered Leader: The First Power of Transformational Leadership* is about elevating your leadership impact.

Are you ready to move beyond leadership skills into leadership transformation? This next book will guide you from insight to influence, connection to transformation, and management to movement-building.

About the Author

Tena H. Sloan is an executive leader, strategist, and consultant specializing in human-centered leadership, emotional intelligence, and organizational transformation. With a rare cross-disciplinary background in both business and mental health, she integrates the art and science of leadership, balancing operational rigor with the deeper work of emotional intelligence and authentic connection. She guides leaders to cultivate self-awareness, strategic clarity, and the capacity to navigate complexity with confidence.

A sought-after speaker, leadership trainer, and consultant, Tena brings a fresh perspective to leadership as a transformational force in organizations and society. *Leadership is Human* is her foundational work, introducing her point-of-view on emotional intelligence and leadership in the age of AI. Blending research, case studies, and actionable frameworks, it challenges outdated leadership models and redefines EQ as the ultimate leadership superpower, helping leaders navigate complexity, inspire trust, and create lasting impact.

Beyond her professional work, Tena is a devoted mother to her daughter, Avery, who inspires her to push beyond limits, embrace possibility, and remain grounded in gratitude. Tena invites leaders to embody their highest vision, break through limitations, and lead with wisdom, presence, and emotional intelligence.

Appendix A
Leadership Action Plan
Step-by-Step Framework for Implementing Emotional Intelligence in Leadership

Emotional intelligence (EQ) is not a theoretical concept —it is a leadership superpower that transforms workplace culture, decision-making, and team dynamics. To help you apply the principles in *Leadership is Human*, this Leadership Action Plan provides a step-by-step framework for integrating emotional intelligence into your daily leadership practices.

Step 1: Assess Your Emotional Intelligence (Self-Awareness & Baseline Measurement)
Before improving EQ, you must understand your current strengths and areas for growth.

Self-Reflection Exercise:

• What are my emotional triggers in leadership?
• How do I typically handle stress, conflict, or setbacks?
• Do my team members feel psychologically safe to express concerns or feedback?

EQ Self-Assessment Questions:

• Do I pause before reacting to difficult situations?
• Can I identify and manage my emotions effectively?
• How often do I seek feedback from my team on my leadership style?

Action Steps:

1. Take an EQ assessment (e.g., *Emotional Intelligence Appraisal* by TalentSmart or Daniel Goleman's EQ framework).
2. Keep a Leadership EQ Journal to track emotions, decisions, and their outcomes.

Step 2: Strengthen Self-Regulation (Managing Emotions & Stress)
Leaders who regulate their emotions create stability in their organizations.

Daily Emotional Check-Ins:

• Identify three emotions you experienced during the day.
• What triggered them, and how did they influence your behavior?

Practical Strategies:

• Implement The Pause Rule – Before responding to an email or conversation, take a moment to breathe and reflect.
• Practice Mindful Leadership – Use deep breathing, meditation, or reflection exercises before high-stakes meetings.
• Develop an Emotional Reset Ritual – Have a go-to strategy for shifting your emotional state when facing challenges (e.g., a 5-minute walk, listening to music, or journaling).

Step 3: Develop Empathy & Active Listening
Empathy is a superpower that builds trust and strengthens relationships.

Empathy Exercises:

• Commit to one daily act of active listening where you listen without interrupting.
• Use the Perspective-Taking Challenge – When engaging with someone, imagine leading from their position.
• Ask open-ended questions: "How do you feel about this?" "What challenges are you facing?"

Action Steps:

1. Schedule empathy check-ins with your team.

2. Implement The Two-Minute Rule – Before responding in a difficult conversation, take two minutes to reflect on what the other person is saying.

Step 4: Master Emotionally Intelligent Communication
Great leaders communicate with clarity, purpose, and emotional awareness.

Practical Strategies:

• Use "I" Statements instead of blame-driven language: "I feel that..." vs. "You always..."
• Read Between the Lines – Observe non-verbal cues, energy shifts, and tone in meetings.
• Practice Reflective Listening – Paraphrase and confirm understanding after key conversations.

Action Steps:

1. Conduct a weekly communication audit – Identify times when your messaging was clear vs. when miscommunication occurred.
2. Improve feedback conversations by focusing on solutions rather than problems.

Step 5: Cultivate Psychological Safety in Your Organization
A culture of psychological safety ensures people feel comfortable expressing ideas, concerns, and challenges.

Leadership Behaviors that Promote Safety:

• Admit mistakes openly to model vulnerability.
• Encourage constructive dissent – Let team members know disagreement is welcome.
• Create structured listening sessions to gather employee perspectives.

Action Steps:

1. Implement a No-Fear Feedback Policy – Make feedback discussions about growth, not punishment.
2. Schedule monthly team reflection sessions on leadership, culture, and innovation.

Step 6: Embed Emotional Intelligence into Decision-Making & Leadership Strategy
EQ should guide strategic choices and leadership decisions.

Decision-Making Strategies:

• Before making a big decision, ask:
• How will this impact my team emotionally and mentally?
• What unintended consequences could arise?
• Use The Leadership Reflection Grid – Weigh decisions against people impact, values alignment, and long-term sustainability.

Action Steps:

1. Apply The 3-Second EQ Rule – Before making any decision, pause for 3 seconds and consider its emotional impact.
2. Start an EQ-Informed Leadership Strategy Session with your executive team.

Step 7: Commit to Continuous EQ Growth
Emotional intelligence is a lifelong leadership practice.

Long-Term Action Steps:

• Enroll in leadership coaching that incorporates EQ.
• Mentor emerging leaders in emotional intelligence.
Engage in a "Leadership EQ Book Club" – Read and discuss books like *Emotional Intelligence 2.0* or *Dare to Lead.*

Reference List

Emotional Intelligence and Leadership Foundations

Bradberry, T., & Greaves, J. (2009). *Emotional intelligence 2.0*. TalentSmart.

Cherniss, C., & Goleman, D. (2001). *The emotionally intelligent workplace: How to select for, measure, and improve emotional intelligence in individuals, groups, and organizations*. Jossey-Bass.

Goleman, D. (1995). *Emotional intelligence: Why it can matter more than IQ*. Bantam Books.

Goleman, D., Boyatzis, R., & McKee, A. (2013). *Primal leadership: Unleashing the power of emotional intelligence*. Harvard Business Review Press.

Menges, J. I., Kilduff, M., Kern, M. C., & Bruch, H. (2015). Emotional intelligence and transformational leadership. *Journal of Applied Psychology, 100*(5), 1300–1313. https://doi.org/10.1037/a0038374

Petrides, K. V., Frederickson, N., & Furnham, A. (2014). Trait emotional intelligence and leadership. *Leadership & Organization Development Journal, 35*(8), 606–624. https://doi.org/10.1108/LODJ-04-2013-0050

Salovey, P., & Mayer, J. D. (1990). Emotional intelligence. *Imagination, Cognition, and Personality, 9*(3), 185–211. https://doi.org/10.2190/DUGG-P24E-52WK-6CDG

Human-Centered Leadership, Psychological Safety, and Workplace Well-being

Brown, B. (2018). *Dare to lead: Brave work. Tough conversations. Whole hearts.* Random House.

Cuddy, A. (2015). *Presence: Bringing your boldest self to your biggest challenges.* Little, Brown and Company.

Edmondson, A. C. (2019). *The fearless organization: Creating psychological safety in the workplace for learning, innovation, and growth.* Wiley.

Grant, A. (2021). *Think again: The power of knowing what you don't know.* Viking.

Kegan, R., & Lahey, L. L. (2009). *Immunity to change: How to overcome it and unlock the potential in yourself and your organization.* Harvard Business Review Press.

Pink, D. H. (2009). *Drive: The surprising truth about what motivates us.* Riverhead Books.

AI, Leadership, and the Future of Work

Deloitte Insights. (2023). *Human-centered leadership in a hybrid world.*

Deloitte. https://www2.deloitte.com/insights

Gallup. (2023). *State of the global workplace report 2023.* Gallup. https://www.gallup.com/workplace

Gartner Research. (2023). *The future of leadership in the age of AI and automation.* Gartner. https://www.gartner.com/en/research

Harari, Y. N. (2023, September). AI, leadership, and the future of decision-making. *The Economist.*

McKinsey & Company. (2024). *The state of AI in 2024.* McKinsey Global Institute. https://www.mckinsey.com/business-functions/ai

World Economic Forum. (2023). *The future of jobs report 2023.* https://www.weforum.org/reports/the-future-of-jobs-report-2023

Emotional Intelligence in Practice: Workplace Case Studies & Thought Leadership

Barsade, S., & O'Neill, O. A. (2016). Manage your emotional culture. *Harvard Business Review, 94*(1), 58–66.

Bersin, J. (2023). The human-centered workplace: How leaders must adapt. *Josh Bersin Academy.* https://www.joshbersin.com

Chamorro-Premuzic, T. (2023, November). Why smart leaders need emotional intelligence more than ever. *Harvard Business Review.* https://hbr.org/2023/11/emotional-intelligence-leadership

Grant, A. (2022, April). The surprising benefits of emotional intelligence in leadership. *Harvard Business Review.*

Harvard Business Review. (2019–2023). *Emotional intelligence series.* Various authors.

NPR. (2023, October). *The science of emotional intelligence and leadership* [Podcast episode]. *Hidden Brain Podcast.*

LEADERSHIP IS HUMAN

The EQ Superpower That Transforms Performance, People, and Impact in the Age of AI

In a world of AI-driven automation and rapid change, one truth remains: the most successful leaders are those who master emotional intelligence (EQ).

Leadership is Human reveals why EQ is the ultimate leadership superpower—the key to outperforming, inspiring, and creating lasting impact. Through research, real-world case studies, and actionable strategies, this book equips leaders to:

- Build trust and psychological safety for high-performing teams.
- Lead with influence, not just authority.
- Navigate uncertainty and change with confidence.
- Leverage EQ as a competitive advantage in the AI era.

For executives, entrepreneurs, and emerging leaders, this is your guide to thriving in the future of leadership—where strategy and technology matter, but human connection matters more.

Master the Leadership Superpower That Sets You Apart.

Because in the Age of AI, Leadership is—and will always be—Human.

www.ingramcontent.com/pod-product-compliance
Lightning Source LLC
Chambersburg PA
CBHW062101270326
41931CB00013B/3165